Jupiter: Gas Giant

Carmel Reilly

AF585429

Jupiter: Gas Giant

Text: Carmel Reilly
Publishers: Tania Mazzeo and Eliza Webb
Series consultant: Amanda Sutera
Hands on Heads Consulting
Editor: Susan Keogh
Project editor: Annabel Smith
Designer: Leigh Ashforth
Project designer: Danielle Maccarone
Illustrations: Nigel Chilvers
Permissions researchers: Lumina Datamatics
Production controller: Renee Tome

Acknowledgements
We would like to thank the following for permission to reproduce copyright material:

Front cover: Science Photo Library - VICTOR HABBICK VISIONS/Brand X Pictures/Getty Images; Title page; p. 4: NASA/GSFC; p. 5: Alan Dyer/Alamy Stock Photo; p. 6: (top) Mopic/Shutterstock.com; back cover; p. 7: Dotted Yeti/Shutterstock.com; p. 9: Nordroden/Shutterstock.com; p. 10: Łukasz Szczepanski/Alamy Stock Photo; p. 11: CBW/Alamy Stock Photo; p. 13: (top) NASA/JPL/Cornell University; (bottom) NASA/JPL/Cornell University; p. 15: NASA/JPL/Cornell University; p. 15 (middle) Science Photo Library/Alamy Stock Photo; p. 16: (top) Joshimer Biñas/Alamy Stock Photo; (bottom) Image Asset Management Ltd./Alamy Stock Photo; p. 17: (top) Science History Images/Alamy Stock Photo; (bottom) RGB Ventures/Alamy Stock Photo; p. 18: Vytautas Kielaitis/Shutterstock.com; p. 19: (top) North Wind Picture Archives/Alamy Stock Photo; (bottom) Photo 12/Universal Images Group/Getty Images; p. 20: (top left) Science History Images/Alamy Stock Photo; p. 21: (top) NASA; (bottom) RUSSELL KIGHTLEY/SCIENCE PHOTO LIBRARY; p. 22: (left) MPI/Archive Photos/Getty Images; (right) NASA Image Collection/Alamy Stock Photo; p. 23: (top left) NASA/SCIENCE PHOTO LIBRARY; (top right) PETER RYAN/SCIENCE PHOTO LIBRARY; (bottom left) NASA Ames; (bottom right) JPL/NASA; p. 24: (top left) NASA/SCIENCE PHOTO LIBRARY; (top right) World History Archive/Alamy Stock Photo; (bottom left) JPL/NASA; (bottom right) NASA/SCIENCE PHOTO LIBRARY; p. 25: (top left) NASA/JPL-Caltech/SwRI/MSSS/Kalleheikki Kannisto; (top right) NASA/JPL-Caltech/SwRI/ASI/INAF/JIRAM; (bottom) NASA/JPL-Caltech/SwRI/MSSS/Betsy Asher Hall/Gervasio Robles; p. 26: (top) NASA/Smithsonian Institution/Lockheed Corporation; (bottom) NASA/ESA/J. Nichols (University of Leicester); p. 27: (top) NASA/ESA/Jupiter ERS Team/Judy Schmidt; (bottom) Science Photo Library/Alamy Stock Photo; p. 28: (top) EUROPEAN SPACE AGENCY/SCIENCE PHOTO LIBRARY; (bottom) NASA/JPL-Caltech/SETI Institute; p. 29: (top) NASA/Kim Shiflett; (bottom) NASA/JPL-Caltech; p. 30: NASA images/Shutterstock.com

Every effort has been made to trace and acknowledge copyright. However, if any infringement has occurred, the publishers tender their apologies and invite the copyright holders to contact them.

NovaStar

Text © 2025 Cengage Learning Australia Pty Limited

Copyright Notice
This Work is copyright. No part of this Work may be reproduced, stored in a retrieval system, or transmitted in any form or by any means without prior written permission of the Publisher. Except as permitted under the *Copyright Act 1968*, for example any fair dealing for the purposes of private study, research, criticism or review, subject to certain limitations. These limitations include: Restricting the copying to a maximum of one chapter or 10% of this book, whichever is greater; Providing an appropriate notice and warning with the copies of the Work disseminated; Taking all reasonable steps to limit access to these copies to people authorised to receive these copies; Ensuring you hold the appropriate Licences issued by the Copyright Agency Limited ("CAL"), supply a remuneration notice to CAL and pay any required fees.

ISBN 978 0 17 033511 9

Cengage Learning Australia
Level 5, 80 Dorcas Street
Southbank VIC 3006 Australia
Phone: 1300 790 853
Email: aust.nelsonprimary@cengage.com

For learning solutions, visit **cengage.com.au**

Printed in China by 1010 Printing International Ltd
1 2 3 4 5 6 7 29 28 27 26 25

Nelson acknowledges the Traditional Owners and Custodians of the lands of all First Nations Peoples. We pay respect to Elders past and present, and extend that respect to all First Nations Peoples today.

Contents

Discovering Jupiter

Jupiter is the fifth planet from the Sun and the largest planet in our solar system. People sometimes call it a “gas giant” because it is mostly made up of gases, and liquids that have formed from gases.

Jupiter is a giant planet and the largest in our solar system.

People have been observing Jupiter from Earth for thousands of years. It is the third-brightest object in our night skies after the Moon and Venus. For a long time, people believed Jupiter was a star. It was only a little over 400 years ago, after the invention of telescopes, that scientists identified Jupiter as a planet.

From Earth, Jupiter looks like a bright star.

Thanks largely to space exploration, we now know a lot about Jupiter. Although people have never visited Jupiter, advances in technology since the 1970s have allowed space organisations to send **uncrewed** spacecraft there on **missions**, or information-gathering voyages. These missions have collected millions of images and large amounts of **data**, which provide us with details about the planet, its **atmosphere** and objects found in the space around it.

Jupiter and Our Solar System

Scientists estimate that our solar system started to form about 4.6 billion years ago. The Sun and then the planets were created over millions of years from a hot spinning disc of gas and dust in a section of the galaxy we call the "Milky Way", which is just one of billions of galaxies in the universe. Jupiter was the first of the planets in our solar system to take shape, forming about 1 million years after the Sun, and about 50 million years before Earth.

Our solar system formed from a hot spinning disc like this.

Key Facts About Jupiter

Scientists have made many discoveries about Jupiter.

- around 86 per cent **hydrogen** gas: what Jupiter is made of, along with **helium** gas (around 13 per cent), and other gases, rock, metal and ice (1 per cent)
- 140 000 kilometres: the distance from one side to the other, going through the middle of Jupiter (on Earth, this distance is about 12 500 kilometres)
- 770 billion kilometres: the distance from the Sun to Jupiter (Earth is only 150 billion kilometres away from the Sun)
- nearly 12 Earth years (11 years, 10-and-a-bit months): the duration of Jupiter's **orbit** (the time it takes to go around the Sun)
- about 9 hours and 50 minutes: the duration of Jupiter's **rotation** or the length of a Jupiter "day" (the time it takes for the planet to completely spin around once)
- 95: the number of moons Jupiter has

Uniquely Jupiter

Jupiter is two-and-a-half times larger than all the other planets in our solar system put together. It is so big that 1300 Earths could be squashed inside it! Jupiter also has the fastest rotation of the planets, making its almost 10-hour-long day the shortest day in our solar system.

Jupiter has many more moons than Earth.

Hot, Hot, Hot ... Cold! Jupiter's Structure

The Surface Gas Layer

The surface layer of Jupiter is largely made up of hydrogen gas, along with helium gas. The temperature is extremely cold, around minus 110 degrees Celsius. Unlike Earth, Jupiter does not have a solid crust, or surface, which means there is nowhere for a spaceship to touch down or for an astronaut to stand.

The Liquid Layer

The liquid layer of Jupiter extends from just below the surface to the top of the inner layer, which is about 7000 kilometres below the surface. It is made up of liquid hydrogen and helium. Temperatures in the liquid layer are about 2000 degrees Celsius.

Jupiter is made up of four different layers.

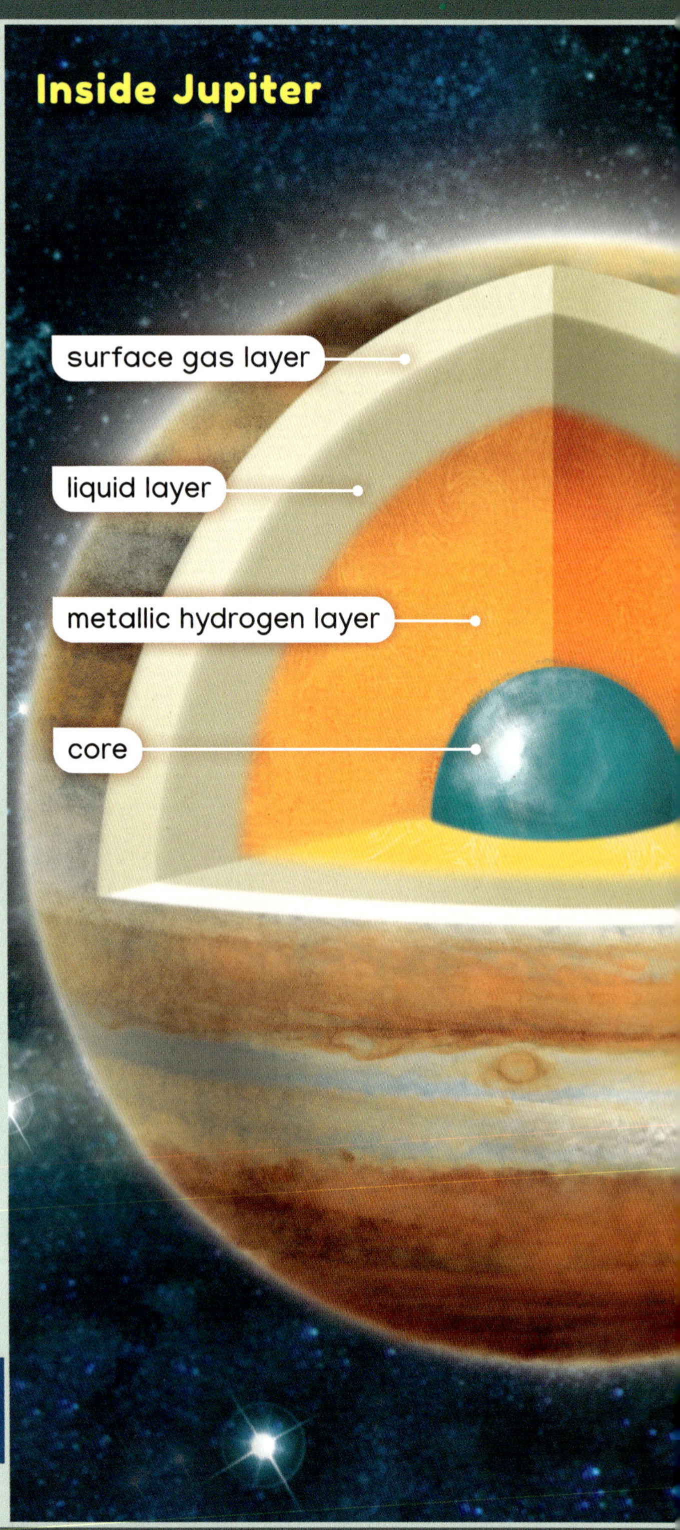

The Metallic Hydrogen Layer

Jupiter has an inner metallic hydrogen layer. This makes up the largest section of the planet. It begins about 14 000 kilometres below the surface and extends down to the core. In this layer, temperatures reach about 5000 degrees Celsius and the hydrogen is in the form of liquid metallic hydrogen.

Core

Jupiter's core, at the centre of the planet, is about 60 000 kilometres below its surface. Scientists are not sure what the core is made from, but most think it is a mixture of rock and metals, and perhaps ice or **metallic hydrogen.** The core could be as hot as 24 000 degrees Celsius – or about four times hotter than the surface of the Sun!

About Hydrogen

Hydrogen is the most plentiful **chemical element** in the universe. Our Sun is about three-quarters hydrogen. Hydrogen is usually a gas. High levels of heat and pressure (a force that pushes against something) will cause the gas to change into a liquid. When pressure and heat increase further, hydrogen changes again into a metallic-like liquid, which is like a **molten** metal.

Heat turns metals into liquids, like this molten gold.

Jupiter's Cloudy Atmosphere

Jupiter's atmosphere begins at the surface gas layer of the planet and stretches about 5000 kilometres out into space. There is not much difference between the planet and its atmosphere, as the atmosphere is made up of up to 90 per cent hydrogen gas and about 10 per cent helium gas. It also contains traces of other gases and ice crystals, which combine to form dense, orange-coloured clouds. These clouds get caught in the planet's rapid rotation and pulled around with it, which is what gives Jupiter its distinctive striped appearance.

Jupiter's fast rotation, along with rising heat from inside, causes powerful air movements in its atmosphere. These, in turn, produce massive storms that we can often see through a telescope from Earth as large swirls or spots of colour. While the lower part of the atmosphere is cool, the upper part of the atmosphere is hotter. This is because the heat from inside the planet rises up. At around 1000 kilometres above the surface gas layer, the temperatures can reach up to 725 degrees Celsius.

Jupiter has distinctive stripes.

The Great Red Spot

The Great Red Spot is a huge storm located in the atmosphere over Jupiter's southern hemisphere. Unlike storms on Earth that only last a few days, storms on Jupiter can last years. The Great Red Spot was first identified by astronomers at least 150 years ago and may have existed for much longer. While scientists are not sure what causes the red colour, they believe it probably comes from the kind of gases that are caught up in it.

The Great Red Storm might be a better name for the Great Red Spot.

Beyond the Atmosphere

Jupiter's Magnetosphere

Jupiter is surrounded by an enormous magnetosphere. A magnetosphere is a bubble-like space around a planet that is formed by that planet's own magnetic field. Magnetic fields are produced by moving **electric charges**. On Jupiter, it is the pressure and constant movement of the metallic hydrogen, along with the planet's rapid rotation, that create these electric charges. The magnetosphere is invisible to the human eye and can only be detected by special equipment.

Most planets in our solar system have their own magnetospheres, but Jupiter's magnetosphere is by far the largest. It is so large that as Jupiter orbits the Sun it has a magnetic tail that stretches almost as far as Saturn! The magnetosphere helps to protect Jupiter from **solar winds** and **space radiation** that, otherwise, would strip away its atmosphere and slowly destroy the planet.

The yellow lines around Jupiter show its large magnetosphere, which helps to protect it.

Jupiter's Rings

While Saturn and Uranus have colourful rings around them that we can see through a telescope from Earth, Jupiter's rings are much fainter and have only been photographed by passing spacecraft. Space scientists think they are made from material knocked from Jupiter's closest moons. This material, made up of rock, ice and dust, then spreads out to form a thin layer, trapped in orbit around the planet.

Jupiter's rings were discovered when they were photographed in 1979.

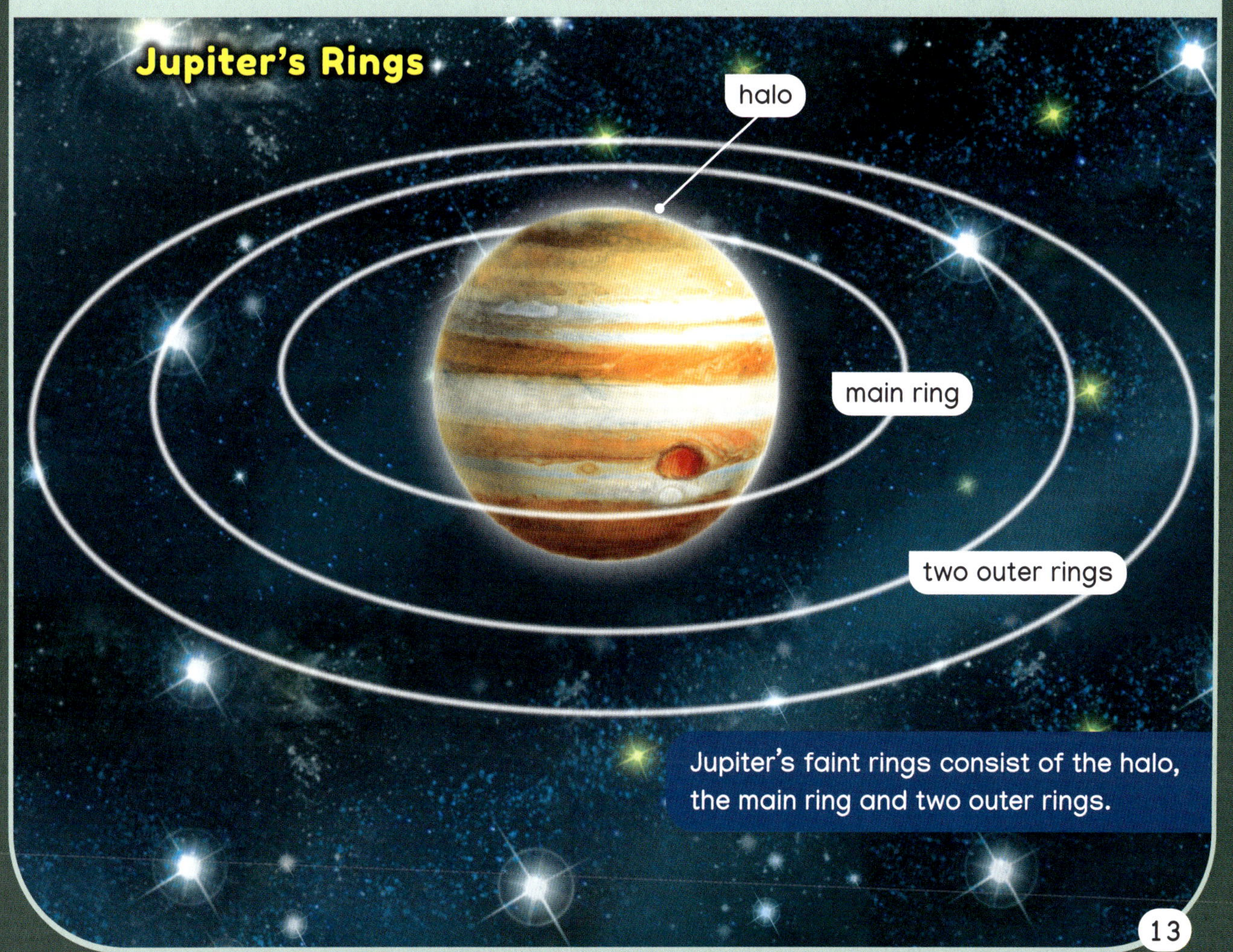

Jupiter's faint rings consist of the halo, the main ring and two outer rings.

Jupiter's Moons

Scientists have identified 95 moons orbiting Jupiter. Unlike Jupiter itself, these moons are not made of gas, but are various combinations of rock, metal and ice. They range in size from thousands of kilometres to just a few kilometres wide or long.

There are three groups of moons: the inner moons, the Galilean moons and the outer moons. The closest of Jupiter's moons only take a few days to orbit the planet while those furthest away can take up to three years. The moons closer to Jupiter orbit in the same anticlockwise direction that the planet rotates in. But most of the outer moons rotate in the opposite direction! Not much is known about these outer moons; some do not even have names.

The Many Moons of Jupiter

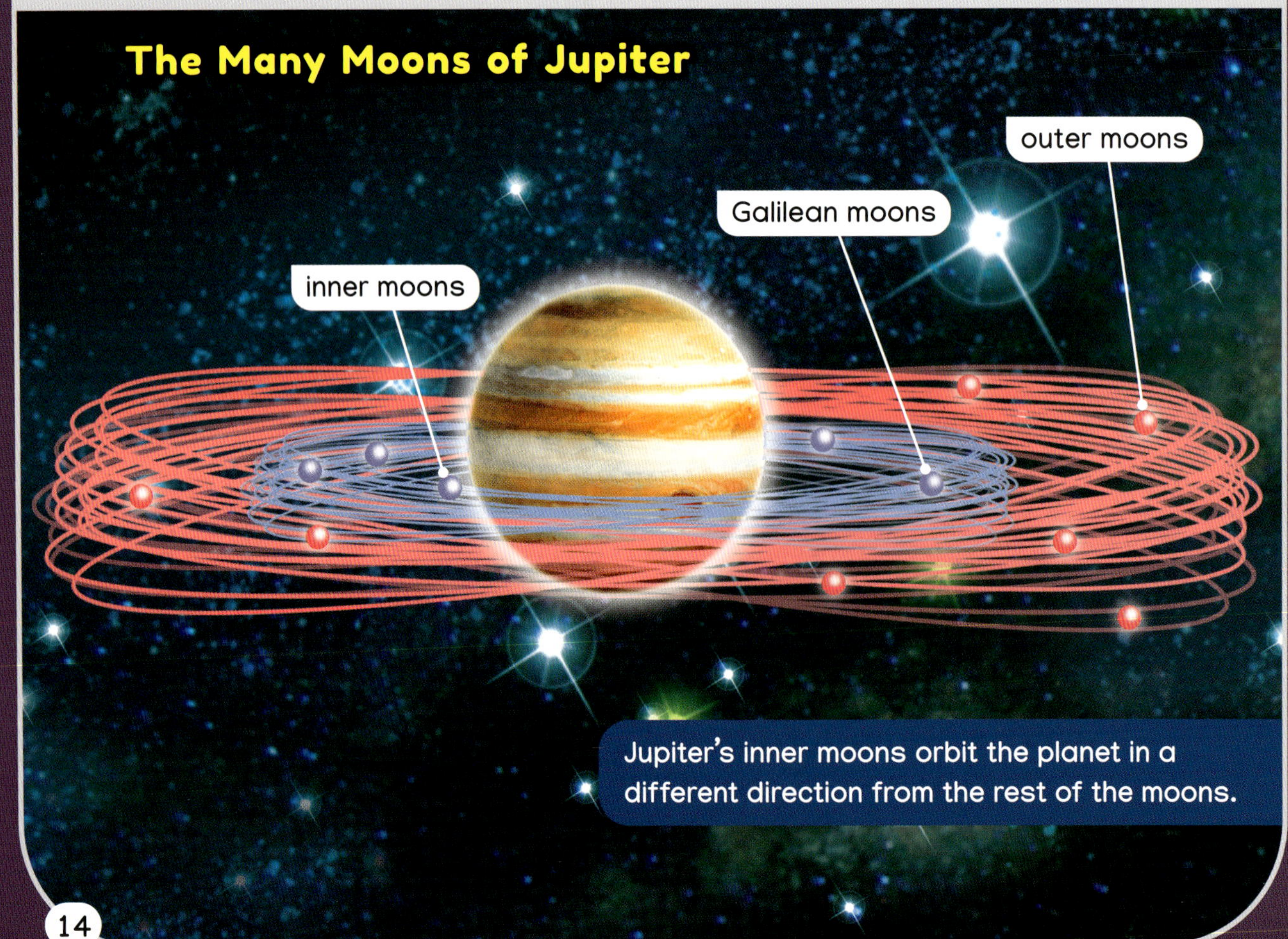

Jupiter's inner moons orbit the planet in a different direction from the rest of the moons.

The Inner Moons

The closest of Jupiter's moons – Metis, Adrastea, Amalthea and Thebe, from nearest to furthest away are four very small, irregularly shaped **cosmic objects** that lie within the planet's rings.

Measuring the Inner Moons

Metis

DISTANCE FROM JUPITER: 128 000 kilometres

SIZE: 43 kilometres (from side to side through its centre)

Adrastea

DISTANCE FROM JUPITER: 129 000 kilometres

SIZE: 16 kilometres (side to side)

Amalthea

DISTANCE FROM JUPITER: 181 000 kilometres

SIZE: 170 kilometres (side to side)

Thebe

DISTANCE FROM JUPITER: 222 000 kilometres

SIZE: 98 km (side to side)

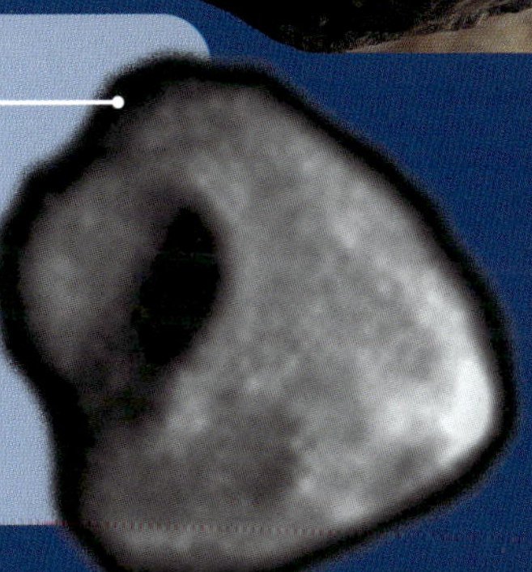

The Galilean Moons

Further out from Jupiter are four large, round moons known as the Galilean moons. These are named after the seventeenth-century Italian astronomer Galileo Galilei, who was the first person to identify them.

Measuring the Galilean Moons

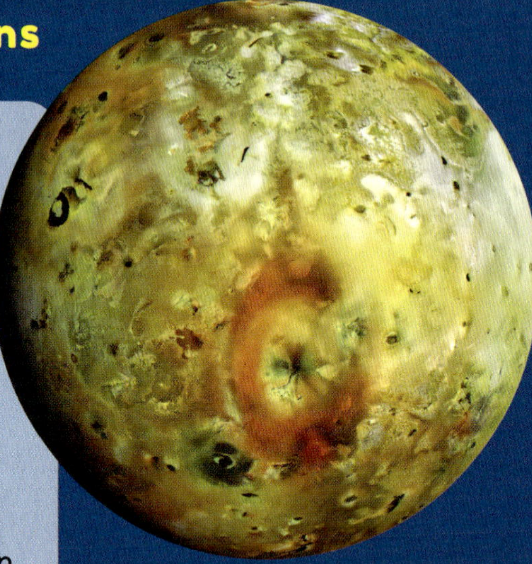

Io

DISTANCE FROM JUPITER: 422 000 kilometres

SIZE: 3640 kilometres
(from side to side through its centre)

Io is the closest large moon to Jupiter. Io is about the same size as Earth's moon, and the distance between Io and Jupiter is similar to the distance between the Earth and the Moon. Io is covered in more than 400 volcanoes and much of its interior is filled with magma, or underground molten rock.

Europa

DISTANCE FROM JUPITER: 671 000 kilometres

SIZE: 3130 kilometres
(from side to side through its centre)

Europa is a very bright moon. This is because the light of the Sun is reflected by its ice-covered crust, which acts like a mirror. Scientists have discovered that an underground sea lies between the moon's crust and its rocky interior. This sea might hold twice as much water as in all of Earth's oceans.

Ganymede

DISTANCE FROM JUPITER: 1 070 000 kilometres

SIZE: 5260 kilometres (from side to side through its centre)

Ganymede is the largest of Jupiter's moons. It is the eighth-largest body in the solar system and is bigger than the planet Mercury! It is made of rock and water and is believed to have an internal ocean. It is the only moon in our solar system to have its own magnetosphere.

Callisto

DISTANCE FROM JUPITER: 1 880 000 km

SIZE: 4820 kilometres (from side to side through its centre)

Callisto is the furthest Galilean moon from Jupiter and the second biggest. Like Ganymede, it is made up of ice and rock, and scientists think it may have an internal ocean. Its surface temperature is about minus 139 degrees Celsius.

Distant Moons

Jupiter's other 87 known moons are very small and lie in very distant orbits, more than 7 million kilometres away from the planet.

Observing Jupiter from Earth

For thousands of years, people have observed Jupiter to help to understand life on our own planet and our place in the universe.

Jupiter and First Nations Peoples

For First Nations peoples, objects in the skies have traditionally been used to tell stories, to help with navigation, and as ways to note the change of seasons and the passing of time. In south-eastern Australia, the Euahlayi/Kamilaroi peoples told a tale that portrayed Jupiter as a boy, wandering away from his mother, the Sun. This reflected the planet's movements at different times of the year. In North America, the arrival of Jupiter in the night sky from May to October traditionally signalled the season of hunting and harvesting.

The brightness of Jupiter has made it easy for people to see it at night for thousands of years.

A Major Discovery

In 1610, the Italian astronomer Galileo Galilei became the first person to identify Jupiter as a planet. After watching Jupiter for some days through a telescope, he realised that there were four cosmic objects orbiting around it. Until then, people had thought that the Sun, Moon, stars and planets had moved while Earth stayed still. But Galileo's observations proved this was not true. This and other later observations he made led to a new understanding of the solar system. Over time it became clear that the Earth and other planets were in fact orbiting around the Sun.

Galileo Galilei

Galileo demonstrated his new invention, the telescope, in Venice.

The Speed of Light

Ole Rømer

Seventeenth-century Danish astronomer Ole Rømer observed Jupiter and its four largest moons through telescopes over many years. He recorded how long it took for each moon to orbit Jupiter and for Jupiter to orbit the Sun. In 1676, he used the data he collected about their orbits to work out the speed of light. The speed of light is the fastest speed anything can travel in space. Knowing this allows us to calculate distances in the universe.

Travel Time

The closest distance between Earth and Jupiter is 588 million kilometres. Today, the fastest spacecraft journey between the two is about 51 days. If we travelled at the speed of light, the trip would be about 40 minutes.

The Speed of Light

EARTH TO MERCURY: 5 light minutes or 15 days by rocket

EARTH TO THE SUN: 8 light minutes or 25 days by rocket

EARTH TO JUPITER: 35 light minutes or more than 3 months by rocket

EARTH TO THE EDGE OF THE SOLAR SYSTEM: 1 light year or 40 years by rocket

The speed of light is the fastest speed in the universe.

Radio Signals

In 1955, American astronomers Bernard Burke and Kenneth Franklin gathered information about **radio transmission signals** from space. They used a field full of **radio antennas** organised in a giant X shape, a design worked out by an Australian astronomer, B.Y. Mills. After some months, Burke and Franklin were surprised to find that Jupiter was one of the strongest sources of radio signals. This led to the discovery of Jupiter's large magnetic fields and magnetosphere. The data Burke and Franklin collected also allowed them to work out the exact length of a day on Jupiter.

This field full of radio antennas picked up signals from radiation on Jupiter.

Magnetospheres radiate energy, and the radio waves in that energy can be detected by sensitive antennas on Earth.

Journeys to Jupiter: A Timeline

People have never travelled further into space than to the Moon. But since the early 1970s, NASA (National Aeronautics and Space Administration) and other space exploration organisations have still managed to visit many parts of our solar system. They have done this by launching uncrewed spacecraft, which are controlled by space scientists on the ground. A number of these spacecraft have visited Jupiter. Today, most of what we know about Jupiter comes from the photographs and data samples taken on these missions.

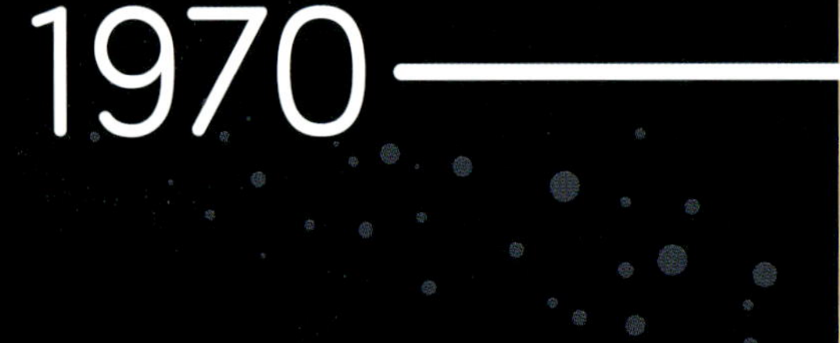

1970

Pioneer 10, launched 1972

Pioneer 10 was the first spacecraft sent to the outer planets by NASA. It arrived near Jupiter in 1973 and spent about three months gathering information on the planet's atmosphere and magnetosphere.

The Pioneer 10 spacecraft is launched.

This is the first "close-up" photograph of Jupiter's moon, Ganymede, taken by Pioneer 10.

Pioneer 11 is checked during construction.

Mission Control is responsible for operating Voyager 1 in space.

Pioneer 11, launched 1973

Pioneer 11 flew by Jupiter in July 1984. It was the first spacecraft to take photos of three of the planet's four Galilean moons. It also took hundreds of pictures of Jupiter and its Great Red Spot.

This is a photograph of Jupiter taken by Pioneer 11.

Voyager 1, launched 1977

Voyager 1 was the first spacecraft to photograph a thin dust ring around Jupiter when it flew near the planet in March 1979. It also identified two new inner moons, Thebe and Metis. It took clear photos of Jupiter's larger moons, showing their surfaces. In these images, scientists could see at least eight active volcanoes on Io.

A volcano erupting on Io, one of Jupiter's moons, was photographed by Voyager 1.

Voyager 2 took this heat-map image of red-hot Io.

The Galileo spacecraft caught this volcanic eruption on Io.

1980

Voyager 2, launched 1977

Voyager 2 reached Jupiter in July 1979. It gathered information on the planet's clouds, moons and rings, and identified the moon Adrastea for the first time. Its cameras took 17 000 pictures, which helped scientists to map out the surfaces of Ganymede and Callisto. Photos taken of Jupiter's surface and the Great Red Spot showed that the storm had changed position, size and colour since Voyager 1 had passed four months earlier.

Galileo, launched 1989

In July 1995, Galileo became the first spacecraft to go into orbit around Jupiter. It passed closer to the planet and many of its moons than any other spacecraft had done. Some of its discoveries included finding a liquid ocean under Europa's surface and a magnetic field around Ganymede. It also mapped Jupiter's vast magnetosphere.

Voyager 2's photographs showed changes in the Great Red Spot.

This close-up photograph of Ganymede was taken by Juno.

Swirling cyclones at Jupiter's north pole were photographed by Juno.

2000

Juno, launched 2011

Juno began orbiting around Jupiter in 2016 and will remain there until at least 2025, exploring as much as possible beneath the planet's dense clouds. Since its arrival, it has photographed Jupiter's north and south poles for the first time and discovered they are surrounded by **permanent cyclones.** It also closely observed the magnetosphere, noting its large, uneven and constantly changing shape.

This is not an eyeball but the surface of Europa, as photographed by the Galileo spacecraft.

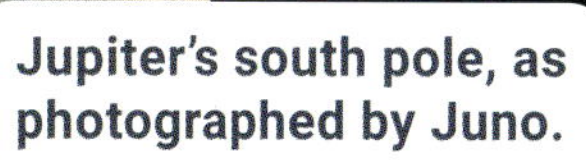

Jupiter's south pole, as photographed by Juno.

Knowledge and Exploration Now and into the Future

Knowledge of Jupiter will only continue to grow as improvements to telescopes and spacecraft help scientists to explore the outer areas of our solar system. Better technology will allow instruments carried by spacecraft to operate in harsh environments and collect data that is hard to access, such as from extremely hot or cold places.

The Hubble Space Telescope is launched into space from the Space Shuttle Discovery.

Exploration Now

NASA's Juno mission is still collecting data and the spacecraft is expected to remain in Jupiter's orbit until at least 2025. Among other things, scientists hope Juno will be able to find out how much water is in Jupiter's atmosphere and to discover what the planet's core is really made from.

Scientists also regularly make observations of Jupiter and the space around it with telescopes and radio telescopes. While most telescopes observe planets from Earth's surface, two are actually in space. The Hubble Space Telescope, a joint project by NASA and the European Space Agency, has been in orbit around Earth since 1990. It observes Jupiter and other planets every year, noting any changes.

A Hubble telescope photograph uses ultraviolet light to detect auroras (shown in blue) at Jupiter's North Pole.

The James Webb Space Telescope, which was built by NASA, the European Space Agency and the Canadian Space Agency, is more modern and powerful than the Hubble. Launched in 2021, it orbits the Sun between Earth and Mars. It has the latest technology, such as special **infrared** cameras, that helped scientists to make three-dimensional models of Jupiter's clouds. Scientists also discovered a very fast wind, what we call a "jet stream" on Earth, blowing over the top of Jupiter's cloud band when they analysed the telescope's images.

This is what Jupiter looks like in infrared photographs.

Information from the James Webb telescope helps scientists to imagine what Jupiter's clouds might look like.

James Webb

The James Webb telescope has taken exceptionally clear photographs of Jupiter. In 2023, images revealed changes in Jupiter's atmosphere that could not be seen in regular photographs.

Exploration into the Future

The JUICE, or Jupiter Icy Moons Explorer, is a spacecraft that was launched in 2023 by the European Space Agency. As it is also travelling to the Sun and Venus, it will not reach Jupiter until 2031. Once there, it will make observations of Jupiter, and the moons Europa, Ganymede and Callisto. Scientists are interested in the possibility that there may be life forms in the moons' under-surface seas.

The JUICE spacecraft is tested before launch.

Scientists hope to find out if the seas under Europa's ice surface contain any life.

The NASA spacecraft Europa Clipper, launched in October 2024, will arrive at Jupiter's fourth-largest moon in 2030. It will look closely at the structure of Europa and the quality of its water, with the idea that perhaps, one day, people could live or work there.

The China National Space Administration is also planning to explore Jupiter, Ganymede and Callisto in a mission called Tianwen-4 in the early 2030s.

The Europa Clipper is unpacked at the Kennedy Space Center in Florida in the USA.

In the future, humans in a space station on Europa may look out and see a view like this as Jupiter rises over the horizon.

Jupiter and Beyond

Space technology has provided us with a great deal of information about Jupiter. We know what it is made from, what its atmosphere is like, that it has a magnetosphere – or invisible force – around it and that it has almost 100 moons! We've discovered that, while life could not exist on Jupiter, scientists are investigating if life may exist in the underground waters of one of its moons. By exploring this hydrogen-rich gas giant we now have a better understanding of not just of Jupiter itself, but our solar system and the universe beyond.

Technology like the Juno spacecraft has enabled scientists to explore Jupiter despite its distance from Earth.

Glossary

atmosphere (*noun*) the gases above the surface of a planet

chemical element (*noun*) one of the different basic substances from which everything is made

cosmic objects (*noun*) things in the universe, such as stars, planets, moons and comets

cyclones (*noun*) low-pressure weather systems that produce storms on both Earth and Jupiter

data (*noun*) facts or information

electric charges (*noun*) being positive or negative due to losing or gaining electrons, one of the structural parts that all substances have

helium (*noun*) one of the simplest basic substances that usually exists as a gas

hydrogen (*noun*) the simplest of all basic substances, made up of just two structural parts; it usually exists as a gas

infrared (*adjective*) a type of light that feels warm but can't be seen

metallic hydrogen (*noun*) liquid hydrogen that behaves like a metal, so it can carry electricity from one point to another

missions (*noun*) expeditions to gather information

molten (*adjective*) melted into a liquid

orbit (*noun*) a circular or oval path that goes right around something, such as a moon around a planet

permanent (*noun*) existing forever

radio antennas (*noun*) special rods that pick up radio waves, and pass them to computers to turn into sounds or images

radio transmission signals (*noun*) sounds and images put into radio waves that can be received and seen or heard by particular machines

rotation (*noun*) to spin completely around; a day is the time it takes for a planet to make one full rotation

solar winds (*noun*) streams of charged particles, caused by enormous heat breaking up chemical elements, erupting out from the Sun

space radiation (*noun*) intense energy, such as x-rays, given off in space by particles like those found in solar winds

uncrewed (*noun*) without any people onboard

Index